In the Wake of War: Improving U.S. Post-Conflict Capabilities

In the Wake of War: Improving U.S. Post-Conflict Capabilities

Report of an Independent Task Force

Sponsored by the Council on Foreign Relations

Founded in 1921, the Council on Foreign Relations is an independent, national membership organization and a nonpartisan center for scholars dedicated to producing and disseminating ideas so that individual and corporate members, as well as policymakers, journalists, students, and interested citizens in the United States and other countries, can better understand the world and the foreign policy choices facing the United States and other governments. The Council does this by convening meetings; conducting a wide-ranging Studies program; publishing *Foreign Affairs,* the preeminent journal covering international affairs and U.S. foreign policy; maintaining a diverse membership; sponsoring Independent Task Forces; and providing up-to-date information about the world and U.S. foreign policy on the Council's website, www.cfr.org.

The Council will sponsor an Independent Task Force when (1) an issue of current and critical importance to U.S. foreign policy arises, and (2) it seems that a group diverse in backgrounds and perspectives may, nonetheless, be able to reach a meaningful consensus on a policy through private and nonpartisan deliberations. Typically, a Task Force meets between two and five times over a brief period to ensure the relevance of its work.

Upon reaching a conclusion, a Task Force issues a report, and the Council publishes its text and posts it on the Council website. Task Force reports reflect a strong and meaningful policy consensus, with Task Force members endorsing the general policy thrust and judgments reached by the group, though not necessarily every finding and recommendation. Task Force members who join the consensus may submit additional or dissenting views, which are included in the final report. "Chairmen's Reports" are signed by Task Force chairs only and are usually preceded or followed by full Task Force reports. Upon reaching a conclusion, a Task Force may also ask individuals who were not members of the Task Force to associate themselves with the Task Force report to enhance its impact. All Task Force reports "benchmark" their findings against current administration policy in order to make explicit areas of agreement and disagreement. The Task Force is solely responsible for its report. The Council takes no institutional position.

For further information about the Council or this Task Force, please write to the Council on Foreign Relations, 58 East 68th Street, New York, NY 10021, or call the Director of Communications at 212-434-9400. Visit our website at www.cfr.org.

Task Force Co-Chairs

Samuel R. Berger
Samuel R. Berger

Brent Scowcroft
Brent Scowcroft

Project Director

William L. Nash
William L. Nash

Task Force Members

Frederick D. Barton

Peter D. Bell*

Samuel R. Berger

Henry S. Bienen

Hans Binnendijk

Antonia Handler Chayes*

Jock Covey*

Ivo H. Daalder*

James F. Dobbins*

Shepard L. Forman*

Bob Graham

Chuck Hagel

John J. Hamre

Jane Harman

Robert D. Hormats

David A. Lipton

William L. Nash

Susan E. Rice*

David Rieff

Kenneth Roth*

Eric P. Schwartz

Brent Scowcroft

Michael A. Sheehan

Walter B. Slocombe*

Gordon R. Sullivan

Mona K. Sutphen

Fareed Zakaria

*The individual has endorsed the report and submitted an additional or a dissenting view.

Working Group Members

Nora J. Bensahel

Evelyn N. Farkas

Victoria K. Holt

Jeff Kojac

Michael Pan

Contents

Foreword

Two years after the United States invaded Iraq, the turmoil there is a daily reminder that winning a war also requires winning the peace. A dramatic military victory has been overshadowed by chaos and bloodshed in the streets of Baghdad, difficulty in establishing security or providing essential services, and a deadly insurgency. The costs—human, military, economic—are high and continue to mount.

For some years, foreign policy experts have debated the desirability and necessity of intervening in "internal" conflicts. In today's world of failed states, terrorism, proliferation, and civil conflict, the trend is clear: The United States will often be drawn into complex situations when they affect its national security or its conscience. Without improved capacities and better organization, the United States will waste time, energy, and critical resources putting together ad hoc responses that may imperil military gains.

This Task Force calls on the president to make improving America's post-conflict reconstruction and stabilization capabilities a top foreign policy priority. The report also puts forward a number of specific recommendations for how best to do so.

Improving America's ability to undertake post-conflict peacekeeping activities should not be mistaken for a commitment to more frequent or unilateral intervention. Rather, recognizing the need to get our own house in order will make our efforts in this area effective if, and when, the United States decides to intervene.

I am grateful for the insights and broad experience of former national security advisers Samuel R. Berger and Brent Scowcroft, two distinguished public servants who continue to enliven foreign policy discussions through endeavors like this Task Force. I also appreciate the efforts of Project Director William L. Nash and the willingness of all the members of the Task Force to make themselves available for this undertaking.

Richard N. Haass
President
Council on Foreign Relations
July 2005

Acknowledgments

As co-chairs of this Task Force, Samuel R. Berger and Brent Scowcroft, brought extraordinarily rich insights to a subject that confounds the most seasoned and adept foreign policy players. Both recognize the importance of finding a better way to define and organize the complex issues associated with post-conflict stabilization and reconstruction. Their ability to forge a consensus is a reflection of their immense experience and remarkable service to the United States. It was an honor to serve under their leadership.

We were privileged to benefit from an extraordinary set of Task Force members and observers. Their diversity of perspective, drawn from experience in government, international organizations, humanitarian agencies, academia, and business, fueled a lively debate over the course of four separate meetings. The report reflects their efforts and expertise.

The co-chairs and I are also very grateful to Lee Feinstein and Eric P. Schwartz, who made important contributions to the drafting of the report. The Task Force also benefited greatly from a separate working group that formulated drafts for Task Force discussions. Mona K. Sutphen, my deputy project director, was the lead drafter of the report. Her intellect, energy, and enthusiasm carried the day. I will be forever grateful for her wit, wisdom, good humor, and forbearance.

Many staff members of the Council on Foreign Relations also deserve recognition. Of first order was the extraordinary work of Amelia Branczik, who served as the research associate for this project in addition to her position as head research associate for the Center for Preventive Action. I am thankful for the efforts of Amanda Raymond, Maria Kristensen, Lindsay Workman, and Jamie Ekern. Richard N. Haass, president of the Council on Foreign Relations, was unwavering in his support and continued his habit of asking hard questions. Special thanks goes to Irina Faskianos, vice president of National Program and Academic Outreach, who organized a series of membership meetings in Atlanta and Chicago on this subject and included the Task Force in this year's national conference.

Finally, the co-chairs and the Task Force would also like to express deep gratitude to the United Nations Foundation, Fundación Juan March, and Fondation pour la Science et la Culture, whose generous financial support made this important project possible.

William L. Nash
Project Director

Task Force Report

Introduction

From Mogadishu to Mosul, the United States has undertaken six major nation-building operations around the world since 1993. The challenges of terrorism, failed states, and proliferation indicate this trend will only continue. Today, in Iraq, the United States carries the bulk of the nation-building burden. Some 135,000 U.S. troops remain on the ground, at an approximate cost of $50 billion per year. Nearly four years after forcing out the Taliban in Afghanistan, 9,000 NATO forces and 17,000 U.S. troops remain in that country to secure the peace and continue the hunt for al-Qaeda.

The pace of peacekeeping activities by the United Nations (UN) and regional organizations also continues to surge, despite the fact that the number of conflicts worldwide has diminished over the past decade. The UN today deploys 67,000 peacekeepers in sixteen operations around the world. With the expected expansion of operations in Africa, these blue-helmeted operations are likely to return to the peak levels of the period following the Cold War.

To succeed, initial military combat operations require advance planning and a substantial commitment of money and manpower. The same is true for the subsequent phase of conflict, commonly called nation-building, and known inside the Pentagon as "stabilization and reconstruction." The failure to take this phase of conflict as seriously as initial combat operations has had serious consequences for the United States, not just in Iraq but, more broadly, for international efforts to stabilize and rebuild nations after conflict.

Violence or instability following the official end of conflict can impose substantial new and even dire challenges on the international community. The failure to implement a comprehensive post-conflict rebuilding effort in Afghanistan following the Soviet withdrawal in 1989 is often cited for its far-reaching consequences. It created a power and security vacuum that, exploited by warlords, ultimately gave sanctuary to the Taliban, Osama bin Laden, and al-Qaeda.

In Iraq, pre-war inattention to post-war requirements—or simply misjudgments about them—left the United States ill-equipped to address public security, governance, and economic demands in the immediate aftermath of the conflict, seriously undermining key U.S. foreign policy goals and giving early impetus to the insurgency.

The Independent Task Force on U.S. Post-Conflict Capabilities has undertaken this study to assess the progress of the United States in developing a civilian and military capacity to meet the demands of stabilization and reconstruction. In undertaking this effort, the Task Force has concluded that the magnitude of the commitment required by Iraq may be unique but the demand for properly trained and equipped military and civilian personnel to stabilize and rebuild nations is not. Failing states or those that are emerging from conflict will remain a significant feature of the international landscape for the foreseeable future, as will the corresponding demand for the United States and others to address this problem.

Defining the Problem

Defining the scope of nation-building is itself a challenge. Stabilization and reconstruction operations straddle an uncomfortable perch between conventional war-fighting and traditional development assistance, both of which—and particularly the former—the United States can do well.

These operations require a mix of skills and training addressing a range of issues, including establishing public security and the rule of law, facilitating political transitions, rebuilding infrastructure, and jumpstarting economic recovery. To complicate matters, stabilization and reconstruction missions must operate in far more demanding—

and often hostile—environments than do traditional economic development programs. And they face narrow windows of opportunity to produce results and convince local populations of the dividends of peace.

Stabilization and reconstruction encompasses military and civilian activities across the full spectrum of a conflict. Different agencies and institutions will play different roles at different stages of a transition. The armed forces will necessarily play a lead role in providing initial security. As security improves, civilian agencies and international financial institutions will move to the forefront. At all stages, close coordination between military and civilian agencies is essential to success, which may be judged by the development of an indigenous capacity for securing essential services, a viable market economy, and self-determination in a healthy civil society. Of course, the best way to address the potential for conflict in weak states may be diplomacy and development assistance.

The Stakes for the United States

After more than a decade of controversy, beginning with the effort by President George H. W. Bush to prevent mass starvation in Somalia, the debate about the importance of peace and stability operations to U.S. security seems to be resolved at the level of stated policy, if not yet in terms of policy implementation.

For over a decade, nation-building has been a controversial proposition. Even today, the term carries negative connotations. The end of the Cold War, and the ability of the members of the United Nations to use the tools of collective security to reverse Iraq's aggression against Kuwait in the first Gulf War, created considerable optimism about the capacity of UN members to address issues of international and internal conflict. In the aftermath of the first Gulf War and throughout the 1990s, the United States led or supported interventions designed to restore internal stability and political reconciliation in Somalia, Cambodia, Haiti, Bosnia and Kosovo, and East Timor, among other places. Few of these interventions can be defined as completely successful. Each has been the subject of negative critiques, which combined to further fuel a contentious debate about the merits of responding to conflict in weak and failing states. On the other hand, proponents argued that the failure to act responsibly led to far worse consequences, such as the Srebrenica massacre and Rwanda genocide.

The parameters of the discussion changed dramatically following September 11, 2001. No longer were the problems presented by failing states viewed simply as a humanitarian concern. As President George W. Bush said in his administration's seminal National Security Strategy of 2002, "The events of September 11, 2001, taught us that weak states, like Afghanistan, can pose as great a danger to our national interests as strong states. Poverty does not make poor people into terrorists and murderers. Yet poverty, weak institutions, and corruption can make weak states vulnerable to terrorist networks and drug cartels within their borders." Action to stabilize and rebuild states marked by conflict is not "foreign policy as social work," a favorite quip of the 1990s. It is equally a humanitarian concern and a national security priority.

Assessing and Addressing the Need

The higher priority now accorded to nation-building has yet to be matched by a comprehensive policy or institutional capacity within the U.S. government to engage successfully in stabilization and reconstruction missions.

Despite some welcome initial moves, responsibility within the U.S. government for stabilization and reconstruction operations is diffuse and authority is uncertain. Policies delineating the proper role of the military and civilian agencies have yet to be articulated. Further, the civilian agencies involved in stabilization and reconstruction activities operate without the benefit of a "unified command" structure ensuring that policy, programs, and resources are properly aligned.

The following pages outline a series of recommendations for how the United States can and should go further to organize itself more effectively and efficiently to undertake stabilization and reconstruction operations, in cooperation with international organizations, regional organizations, and foreign governments.

We Are in This Together

The focus of the report is the capacity of the U.S. government, but the mechanisms by which the United States interacts with multilateral and regional organizations are also an important component and therefore are addressed in this report.

Successful stabilization and reconstruction operations require a range of skills and expertise and exact a heavy price that no single nation can easily assemble or afford. In countries where active conflict has largely abated but instability remains, UN-led operations are generally the most cost-effective means to promote both the effective involvement of the international community and long-term security and stability. The $4 billion estimated annual costs of all seventeen ongoing UN-led deployments, of which the United States is responsible for roughly $1.2 billion, is a relative national security bargain. That said, many of the challenges facing the United States, including lack of policy direction, diffuse authority, and duplicative efforts, plague other governments and multilateral and regional organizations.

While the challenge of stabilization and reconstruction must be confronted by the international community as a whole, we focus our attention on the progress needed in the United States. By getting its own house in order, the United States will be in a strong position to persuade others to do so.

Leadership Matters

Start at the Top

The institutional changes recommended in this report cannot be accomplished without high-level attention and support. Throughout its history, the United States has shown itself capable of changing course when there is consensus on the need to do so. With sustained leadership in the executive and legislative branches, substantial progress on this critical national security priority can and must occur in the months and years ahead.

After the attacks of September 11, 2001, the president acknowledged the national interests at stake when failed states are left to fester. The remaining second-term task is to institutionalize this policy. To that end, *the Task Force calls on the president to make clear that building America's capability to conduct stabilization and reconstruction operations will be a top foreign policy priority. This proposition requires the necessary legislation and additional resources.*

Today, as in the past, no arm of the U.S. government is formally in charge of post-conflict stabilization and reconstruction overseas. Policy and implementation are divided among several agencies, with poor interagency coordination, misalignment of resources and authorities, and inadequate accountability and duplicative efforts.

This absence of an institutional framework reflects an outdated and wishful attitude that stabilization and reconstruction operations are extraordinary rather than routine.

Early nation-building efforts in Haiti, Somalia, and the Balkans began as though they were the first of their kind. By the mid-1990s, the U.S. government began to codify lessons learned and improve planning for subsequent operations. Unfortunately, the lessons of the 1990s were disregarded in the planning for Afghanistan and Iraq. The result has been inefficient operations, billions of dollars of wasted resources, and stymied ambitions. The United States can no longer afford not to learn from its experience.

The post-conflict situation in Iraq exemplifies this failure. More than two years after a stunning three-week march to Baghdad, the U.S. military and newly trained Iraqi forces have yet to secure the country, and the reconstruction process has fallen victim to this lack of security. As the president said recently, "One of the lessons we learned from our experience in Iraq is that, while military personnel can be rapidly deployed anywhere in the world, the same is not true of U.S. government civilians."[1]

The situation in Iraq has helped mobilize support for institutional change. Independent groups have made thoughtful recommendations on how to change the U.S. approach, and their assessments yield crucial lessons that inform the work of this Task Force.[2] The administration has created the Office of the Coordinator for Stabilization and Reconstruction at the State Department, and the Department of Defense is defining stabilization operations as a core mission. These developments, discussed in more detail below, are welcome first steps.

[1] Remarks by President Bush at the International Republican Institute (IRI) Dinner, Washington, DC, May 18, 2005, PRNewswire.

[2] The Task Force's efforts build on a number of previous studies conducted on post-conflict needs and how these needs should be addressed. A joint project between the Center for Strategic and International Studies (CSIS) and the Association of the U.S. Army (AUSA) entitled "Post-Conflict Reconstruction Task Framework," May 2002, is a comprehensive review of post-conflict reconstruction tasks. Other important studies that this report draws on are: *Play to Win: Report of the Post-Conflict Reconstruction Commission,* January 2003, and *Winning the Peace—An American Strategy for Post-Conflict Reconstruction,* both published by CSIS; *Building Civilian Capacity for U.S. Stability Operations: The Rule of Law Component* by the U.S. Institute of Peace (USIP), Special Report 118, April 2004; *On the Brink: Weak States and U.S. National Security,* by the Center for Global Development; the *Report of the UN Secretary-General's High-Level Panel on Threats, Challenges and Change;* and *America's Role in Nation-Building: From Germany to Iraq* from RAND's National Security Research Division, 2003. Additionally, work by the National Defense University, The Henry L. Stimson Center, and the Panel on UN Peacekeeping Operations, add important contributions to the debate and to this report.

Command and Control

The transition from war to "non-war" and then to stabilization and reconstruction is particularly challenging. It is a "neither fish nor fowl" period, involving political-military considerations that are often contradictory and always complex. Understandably, managing this shift is difficult because the lines of responsibility are often fluid, with an uneasy division between military and civilian authority. This division is not trivial in scope or consequence. Resolving these inevitable conflicts is essential, requiring the highest-level authority to provide guidance, resources, and decisive leadership.

Strengthening this weak link requires better civilian-military coordination of policy matters and ground-level operations. Policymakers have to commit the resources (both in dollars and personnel) needed to achieve the stated policy objectives and operational needs.

The importance of strong leadership in this area cannot be overstated. Policy has to be set clearly, or the United States will continue to struggle with a lack of coherence and bureaucratic chaos at best or mission failure at worst.

In 1997, the Clinton administration attempted to address the issue in the form of Presidential Decision Directive 56 (PDD-56). It outlined the roles and responsibilities of various agencies involved in "complex contingency operations" and reflected many of the lessons learned in the early 1990s. While PDD-56 helped establish a framework for civilian-military coordination, it was never consistently applied. When the second Bush administration came into office, it discarded the directive, reflecting its general skepticism about the interventions undertaken by the Clinton administration.

In the aftermath of the terrorist attacks of September 11, 2001, and the invasion of Afghanistan, the Bush administration suddenly faced many of the challenges of coordination that confronted its predecessor. However, the Bush administration waited until January 2003, while planning for the Iraq War, to issue National Security Presidential Directive-24 (NSPD-24) regarding the question of post-war reconstruction. The directive was immediately controversial. It was issued less than sixty days before the intervention in Iraq and was widely seen as a very late start to a formidable undertaking in post-war planning. More importantly, it broke with tradition and put the Department of Defense in charge of post-war reconstruction planning, conflicting with the sentiments of many administration and Defense Department officials, who argued that civilian agencies are better-placed to take the lead on post-intervention reconstruction. Today, most argue that the Defense Department was not prepared to take on the complex task of post-intervention stabilization and reconstruction in Iraq.

In May 2004, in preparation for the turnover of sovereignty to Iraq, President Bush seemed to recognize the problem and issued a new NSPD on U.S. government operations in Iraq, handing over responsibility for the supervision and general direction of all post-war assistance to the State Department. However, the Defense Department retains control over many aspects of the post-war reconstruction, including police and military training and economic infrastructure rehabilitation. Further, in July 2004 the administration created a new State Department Office of the Coordinator for Reconstruction and Stabilization. This welcome first step is discussed later in this report.

Despite these measures, the United States still lacks an overarching framework to guide stabilization and reconstruction activities across the government. Administration efforts to engage in a new review process for a potential follow-on document to PDD-56 were ultimately shelved because of interagency disagreement.

The National Security Adviser and his staff should be formally tasked with civilian-military coordination and establishing overarching policy associated with stabilization and reconstruction activities. This role should be codified in a new National Security Policy Directive, and knowledgeable, competent personnel assigned to fulfill this mandate.

Given the stakes, the complexity, and the interagency nature of policy decisions associated with stabilization and reconstruction, the National Security Adviser and the National Security Council (NSC) staff needs to formulate policy in this area. The Task Force recommends creating a senior director-level position and associated directorate for stabilization and reconstruction activities. This directorate would be responsible for coordinating mission planning and civil-military relations and for establishing interagency roles and responsibilities. To coordinate mission-specific policy issues, the Deputies Committee could establish interagency executive committees (EXCOMs) composed of appointees from relevant agencies.

The Task Force notes and welcomes the administration's current plan to establish a "Stabilization and Reconstruction Deputies' Coordination Committee," designed to develop general policy in this area. However, the Task Force believes any successful coordination mechanisms need to be institutionalized. This would help avoid the inclination of every new administration to reinvent the wheel.

The Task Force also recommends creating new joint training activities to further civilian–military cooperation in the field. Today, there is almost no opportunity for the military to train alongside civilians with whom they will actually work in operations overseas. *The Defense and State Departments should jointly support an interagency, integrated training program(s) at the National Defense University and the National Foreign Affairs Training Center.* Such a step would better prepare civilians and the military alike and strengthen interagency relationships and awareness.

Military Challenges

War-fighting has two important dimensions: winning the war and winning the peace. The United States excels in the first. But without an equal commitment to stability and reconstruction, combat victories can be lost. The military's bravery, dedication, and skill is unsurpassed, but it must have the institutional and resource support from the U.S. government in order to succeed in securing the peace.

The immediate post–combat phase of war requires a shift in rules of engagement, doctrines, skills, techniques, and perspective appropriate to the mission. Troops are expected to be able to shift from destroying the enemy to engaging the populace, whether monitoring ceasefires, helping maintain public security where local institutions are lacking, or maintaining basic services and infrastructure. In Afghanistan and Iraq, where there is active armed resistance, these tasks require military forces to shift back and forth from combat to stability operations on a moment's notice or conduct both simultaneously.

Notwithstanding these challenges, the military on the ground represents the only capability to manage the impact of a leadership vacuum and head off a rapid spiral into lawlessness and human tragedy. However experienced or talented civilians may be, the military always will have the main responsibility for establishing and maintaining public order, security, and emergency services in an immediate post–combat setting.

Senior officials at the Department of Defense and within the U.S. military have been ambivalent about U.S. military participation in stabilization and reconstruction missions. Many argued that the military's

13

critical mission is war-fighting, defined as combat operations, with little emphasis on post-conflict tasks. In particular, they asserted that UN-style peacekeeping deployments adversely affects combat-readiness. They also complained that the intractable nature of many political conflicts leads to deployments of indefinite duration, compounding problems of readiness, force allocation, and acceptable national risk.

The Bush administration entered office sharing this skepticism. On a number of occasions early in the administration, Secretary of Defense Donald Rumsfeld echoed these traditional reservations. The events of September 11 and the military defeat of the Taliban in Afghanistan did not immediately change the opinion of Department of Defense or military officials on the role of U.S. troops in stabilization operations.

The military's emphasis on high-intensity conflict has produced major benefits. The United States is winning wars faster and with fewer forces and casualties. U.S. forces moved from Kuwait to Baghdad with stunning effectiveness in the spring of 2003. But the American military's successes in combat have had an unintended consequence. Rapid victory collapses the enemy but does not destroy it. Adversaries can go underground to prepare to wage guerilla warfare, creating a need for more troops for longer periods of time during the stabilization and reconstruction phases. This unintended consequence of military "transformation" has important implications for the structure and size of the military.

Current Administration Policy

The experiences of Afghanistan and Iraq have altered policies and attitudes in the Department of Defense and within the military. The change is most evident in the Army and the Marine Corps, as the two services are developing doctrine and extracting lessons learned from these operations. A series of recommendations on stabilization operations also was issued last summer by the Defense Department's Science Board, reflecting concern at the highest levels.

While these are important steps, the overall effort is slow and has yet to be fully accepted throughout the Department of Defense. Moreover, the Defense Department has yet to address a series of critical questions regarding the size and structure of the armed forces. The Task Force addresses several of these issues in the following recommendations.

The president and the secretary of defense firmly establish that stability operations are a strategic priority for the armed forces. Stability and reconstruction needs to be understood and treated as a mission as important to America's security as high-intensity combat operations. For this message to take hold, it must come unambiguously from the top, beginning with the president and reinforced by the secretary of defense. To that end, the secretary of defense should issue immediately a directive that defines stability and reconstruction operations as a core military mission and accords such operations priority and attention comparable to combat operations. Further, the Quadrennial Defense Review, the Strategic Planning Guidance, and the National Military Strategy should be used to further establish such operations as essential tasks.

Right-Size the Force

Acknowledge the breadth and depth of the stabilization mission and plan accordingly, including having the right mix and number of troops to provide for sustained operations.

The Bush administration's defense policies have emphasized high-intensity combat, which has been the focus of Secretary Rumsfeld's policy of military transformation. The strategy outlined in the most recent Quadrennial Defense Review puts as top priorities homeland defense, peacetime deterrence in four regions, and fighting two major conflicts simultaneously. It also calls for the ability to fight one "regional conflict," a capacity the United States has far exceeded with the extended deployments in Afghanistan and Iraq.

The critical miscalculation of Iraq war-planning was that the stabilization and reconstruction mission would require no more forces than the invasion itself.[3] As a result, too few troops were deployed and the

---

[3] See comments made by Secretary of Defense Rumsfeld at a February 27, 2003, Pentagon press conference, http://www.pentagon.mil/transcripts/2003/t02272003_t0227ap.html, and testimony by Deputy Secretary of Defense Paul Wolfowitz and Secretary Rumsfeld before the Defense Subcommittee of the U.S. House of Representatives Appropriations Committee, March 27, 2003.

multiyear deployments in Afghanistan and Iraq have heavily taxed the active duty armed forces and, even more, the National Guard and reserves (which together comprise 40 percent of the troops in the field in Iraq). With the support of Congress, the secretary of defense has temporarily increased the size of the U.S. Army by 30,000 soldiers, to help meet these demands. This was a logical step and needs to become permanent—the size of the U.S. Army (active and reserve) is too small for the missions it has been assigned. But, increasing the number of soldiers alone is insufficient.

The belated recognition of the need for a different skill set to conduct stabilization missions contributed to recent U.S. Army initiatives to convert some artillery and air defense units to military police and civil affairs units. However, the stability mission requires even more adjustment of the force structure and associated training. Knowledge of regions and associated history and customs, language skills, and intelligence and counterintelligence expertise are in great demand, as is the need for more engineers, logistics, and communications personnel.

General Purpose, Not Dedicated Constabulary Forces

Well-grounded concerns about overspecialization, as well as the probable demands of future conflict, lead the Task Force to call for a general purpose force, trained, prepared, and equipped for high-intensity combat and stabilization and reconstruction, rather than establishment of a dedicated constabulary force.

The United States has a long history of using its combat forces in a constabulary role when necessary to provide public security and the rule of law. Opposition to rebuilding a dedicated U.S. constabulary force in the military is strong, even though several European allies—Italy, France, and Spain—are improving the constabulary capabilities in their national police forces. The traditional concern is that dedicated constabulary forces lack the training and experience to engage in high-intensity combat, a capability that is often necessary in an unstable post-intervention setting. In addition, there is concern within the army that a dedicated constabulary force would have trouble attracting quality recruits or would adversely influence recruiting combat forces.

Achieving U.S. wartime aims requires that military forces as well as policy be able to shift rapidly between a high-intensity combat footing and a stabilization role because that is the environment they are most likely to confront in the future.

The Task Force gave careful consideration to calling for the creation of a constabulary-type force. However, given the proposed priority to the stabilization mission and the modifications to the force structure discussed above, the Task Force concluded that the necessary military capability could be achieved by proper doctrine and training adjustments. Recognition of the post-conflict mission and the need to prepare for it was missing from the Iraq war plan. This can be corrected. The U.S. Army has demonstrated on numerous occasions its ability to handle these missions when so directed.

Apply Emerging Technologies

The Defense Department should apply existing and emerging technologies to support stabilization operations in keeping with the elevated status of stabilization missions. This means a general review of the implications of counterinsurgencies for equipment and weapons. Off-the-shelf technologies, including broadband wireless and encrypted satellite-supported cell phones, pre-packaged and ready to deploy, need to be given to military forces. Other technologies applicable to stability operations include vehicle ID tracking, enhanced armored vehicles, biometric identification, and information analysis tools such as elite profiling and collaborative planning tools. Similarly, the Defense Department should apply emerging technologies to this mission, including nonlethal weaponry, stand-off explosive detection equipment, Unmanned Aerial Vehicles (UAVs), and lightweight armor.

Training the Next Generation

The war colleges and staff colleges should develop appropriate educational programs and doctrine to support civilian-led stabilization operations.

The next generation of military officers needs to understand that stabilization is a core mission, not an adjunct to combat. This will require a sharpened mission focus and new operational concepts at all levels of command as well as revision of training programs and professional military education. Steps now underway to develop new operational doctrine for stabilization and reconstruction operations are welcome and should be based on recent as well as historical experience. The ultimate goal is to change the culture of the military and create expertise on how to transition from combat to a public security and reconstruction mission.

Institutional Changes

The Department of Defense should establish senior positions within the Office of the Secretary of Defense and the Organization of the Joint Chiefs of Staff dedicated to the stabilization mission.

At the policy level, the Department of Defense should establish an assistant secretary of defense for stabilization operations. Over the years, stability operations have been treated as orphans within the Office of the Secretary of Defense, often falling to a deputy assistant secretary with little influence over the uniformed military or within the interagency bureaucracy. An assistant secretary of defense position would create a focal point for policy matters associated with post-conflict operations. The assistant secretary would participate in civil-military policy and planning coordination, and work closely with the assistant secretary of defense for special operation and low-intensity conflict.

Similarly, the Defense Department should develop a joint staff capacity to oversee and coordinate military planning for post-conflict stabilization operations. Further, a joint command could develop operational and training doctrine, including training and exercising in stability operations.

The Civilian Challenge

Unity of command among civilian agencies is desperately needed. Today, responsibility for stabilization and reconstruction is dispersed and duplicated across numerous agencies,[4] often leading to overlapping efforts and a lack of coherence in setting priorities and allocating resources. This diffuse authority also limits real accountability.

Follow the Leader

The State Department should lead all civilian efforts related to stabilization and reconstruction, with requisite increases in resources and funding authority for relevant executive branch programs. The United States Agency for International Development should be responsible for managing the daily operations associated with these activities.

---

[4] For example, agencies working on economic reconstruction include the departments of State, through the Bureau of Economic and Business Affairs; Treasury, through the Office of Technical Assistance, which assists in budget policy and management, financial institutions policy and regulation, government debt issuance and management, financial enforcement, and tax policy and administration; Commerce, which, for example, operates the Iraq Investment and Reconstruction Task Force to facilitate business opportunities for U.S. companies in Iraq's reconstruction; USAID, which takes the lead in development programs; and Labor, which has a program to assist rehabilitation of child soldiers. While humanitarian assistance is most commonly associated with USAID, other agencies involved include the Departments of Agriculture through its Foreign Agricultural Service; and Health and Human Services (DHHS) Center for Disease Control's International Emergency and refugee Health Branch. Rule of Law programs are located at USAID's Office of Transition Initiatives and Democracy, Conflict and Humanitarian Assistance, as well as the Department of Justice's Office of International Affairs, responsible for the International Criminal Investigative Training Assistance Program (ICITAP) and the Office of Overseas Prosecutorial Development, Assistance, and Training (OPDAT).

The U.S. government needs a single civilian agency to set priorities, identify the skills needed and where the people with those skills are located, and decide the best way to assemble and deploy these capabilities. This would improve overall effectiveness in managing the myriad civilian programs like police training and rebuilding critical infrastructure, as well as in navigating the overall political dynamics of a particular mission, including shaping the behavior of neighboring states and negotiating both the military, civil, and monetary contributions of other donors and the activities of international organizations like the UN.

The Task Force recommends that the NSC coordinate the civilian-military issues and overarching policy. We further believe that the Department of State must be empowered to manage and oversee *implementation* of policy in this area. The Task Force understands the extent to which this will require fundamental State Department reform. However, no other agency within the U.S. government has the expertise to undertake what is basically an exercise involving state-to-state relations.[5] Further, the State Department is best suited for this role, as it maintains regular contact with all the relevant actors and already is responsible for much of the civilian stabilization and reconstruction effort.

Many Task Force members expressed well-founded concerns about the practical ability of the State Department to oversee effectively the work of USAID and other agencies. However, we concluded that the critical component to achieve success is aligning and streamlining budget authority for stabilization and reconstruction activities at the State Department (discussed further below).

Senators Richard Lugar (R-IN) and Joseph Biden (D-DE) have sponsored legislation, currently pending action by the full Senate, to strengthen the State Department's ability to take on this broader management role. ***The Task Force recommends speedy enactment of this legislation as the foundation for the recommendations below.***

---

[5] This point reinforces a key recommendation outlined in the CFR/CSIS Independent Task Force report on State Department reform, issued in early 2001, available at http://www.cfr.org/pub3890/frank_c_carlucci_jamie_f_metzl/state_department_reform.php.

The Daily Grind

With the Department of State overseeing the civilian effort, **USAID would lead the day-to-day execution of the programs and activities on the ground.** To do this, it must receive greater funding and resources. Through its humanitarian crisis response role, USAID has the experience and expertise to operate field-level programs in difficult operating environments. More than any other agency, USAID is best prepared to handle the logistical, contractual, and administrative aspects of daily stabilization activities. Moreover, stabilization and reconstruction work would reinforce USAID's mission for development and its longer-term efforts to create self-sustaining states. Like the Department of State, USAID faces significant challenges if it is to undertake this expanded role. Congress has cut its budget while adding new priorities to its mandates, constraining its ability to carry out programs effectively.

A Step Forward

The most significant institutional adjustment to date has been the creation in April 2004 of the Office of the Coordinator for Reconstruction and Stabilization at the State Department, which oversees the government's civilian capacity to prevent or prepare for post-conflict crises.[6] It will create a new Active Response Corps intended to speed the deployment of civilians in crises, but the office has not been fully funded nor does it have sufficient personnel for it to fulfill its mandate.[7]

We welcome the creation of this new office. At the same time, we question whether it has the necessary capacity and bureaucratic heft to play a strong interagency management and external coordination role. Of further concern is its exclusion from the Iraq and Afghanistan

[6] Its five functions include: (1) developing policy options and planning to avert or respond to crises; (2) coordinating the deployment of U.S. resources toward post-conflict requirements; (3) establishing and managing interagency capabilities and surge capacity; (4) incorporating best practices and lessons-learned to improve performance; and (5) coordinating with international partners (multilateral organizations, nongovernmental organizations [NGOs], and others). See slides presented by the Coordinator for Stabilization and Reconstruction, Carlos Pascual, at http://www.state.gov/s/crs/rls/37482.htm.

[7] Ramping up the Active Response Corps, to be made up of foreign and civil service officers who can deploy quickly to crisis situations, is contingent on funding requested for FY2006.

missions, and—perhaps most critically—the failure to secure the full funding the office requires.

Elevate and Empower

The State Department coordinator should be elevated to an undersecretary of state–level position. The new undersecretary would have authority over civilian aspects of the stabilization and reconstruction activities, including tasking other agencies with special expertise, and coordinating and directing U.S. government funding. Other civilian agency activities in Washington and in the field would ultimately be subordinate to the undersecretary and, by extension, to senior-level officials appointed by the undersecretary to oversee individual missions. An undersecretary-level position demonstrates the importance of post-conflict reconstruction and stabilization as a core State Department mission, just as arms control and counterterrorism are treated today. While post-conflict efforts would be the first priority, the new undersecretary would also be the lead player in the State Department for conflict prevention and mitigation efforts.

A significant reserve or contingency fund should be established for this office to be used for crises or other unanticipated demands. The 2006 budget request currently includes $100 million for a Conflict Response Fund. This is a welcome first step, but the Task Force believes the fund should be enhanced to enable quick and effective response to post-conflict situations.[8] The Task Force calls on the Office of Management and Budget and Congress to create a replenishing reserve fund of $500 million to support the work of the new undersecretary, including both the development of new capabilities within the U.S. government and implementation of prevention and stability and reconstruction programs. Current funding for stabilization and reconstruction activities should be combined, creating a single, flexible, "no year" account of sufficient size that would ease reliance on supplemental appropriations to handle crises. Providing this authority within a single spending line

---

[8] President Bush's May 18, 2005, remarks to IRI.

was proposed by Senators Lugar and Biden in 2004 and would give the undersecretary the needed agility and authority to ensure U.S. policies, responses, and programs are effectively coordinated, timely, and consistent with U.S. foreign policy goals. The Task Force believes that empowering the State Department to oversee programs across the executive branch will help resolve bureaucratic rivalries that now constrain effective coordination and waste time and money.

Improve the Ground Game

The State Department should deploy as early as possible civilian "advance teams" to work alongside the military, down to the brigade level. Such a step would help promote civilian-military coordination and streamline the often awkward transition from primarily military-led activities to civilian-directed efforts. Further, this would facilitate the flow of crucial information about developments on the ground. Over time, as the security environment allows, the civilian staffing would increase and the military presence would be drawn down.

The State Department should create a new unit, reporting to the undersecretary, to further streamline and promote public security and rule of law programs. The United States has consistently failed to deploy international civilian police quickly in the aftermath of conflict, and has resorted to over-reliance on an ill-prepared military to address policing tasks. Also, the government's effort to prepare a cadre of trained civilian government employees and volunteers for participation in stabilization operations has been inadequate, despite strong U.S. rhetorical support for such training. The lack of public security capability is one of the most serious gaps in U.S. capacity.

Authority for the civilian dimensions of public security and the rule of law has been dispersed among U.S. government agencies.[9]

---

[9] There was an attempt to address this issue in February 2000, when President Clinton signed PDD-71, "Strengthening Criminal Justice Systems in Support of Peace Operations," which urged the State Department to take the lead in improving the recruitment and training of U.S.-supplied civilian police, and to undertake a range of activities in support of the rebuilding of foreign criminal justice systems. However, implementation of the directive was weak, and the PDD was not formally endorsed by the Bush administration.

Recruitment and deployment of U.S. civilian police is a joint responsibility of the Department of State and the Department of Justice, with rule-of-law assistance carried out among a number of U.S. government offices.

These programs should be consolidated at the Department of State with an attendant increase in resources for the department. The current international civilian police (CIVPOL) program[10] should be reorganized and expanded to include a core force of several hundred full-time officers,[11] deployable on an immediate basis. In addition, the new CIVPOL operation should seek to develop a reserve roster of up to 4,000 trained officers who could be mobilized to participate in post-intervention missions. A top priority will be finding experts who are fluent in local languages and understand the culture and politics.

A Judicial Corps team should be established to develop rosters of pre-qualified and trained human rights monitors, judges, court staff, attorneys, and corrections officers, who would be available and prepared to deploy on short notice. The Judicial Corps would also assist in war crimes investigations. In addition, criminal justice training programs now housed at the Department of Justice[12] would be transferred to the State Department and broadened in areas relating to local law enforcement (e.g., police and prosecutor training, anti-corruption efforts, community policing, and penal reform).

Create a Deputy Administrator for Stabilization and Reconstruction Operations at USAID. The new deputy administrator would report

[10] The existing CIVPOL program, located within the International Narcotics and Law (INL) Enforcement Affairs bureau at State, recruits U.S. police officers who undertake typical policing tasks (e.g., "beat cops"), often within a UN-managed program. Currently, the CIVPOL program is managed primarily by private contractors, but in an expanded program, management should revert back to the U.S. government directly (though subcontracting for training and support of the program could remain in place).

[11] These officers could be full-time federal government personnel or within a new federal-state partnership, as recommended by the U.S. Institute of Peace, whereby the Federal Government would pay a large percentage of officers' salaries, and those officers would be "on call" for deployments overseas. For more explanation, see: USIP Special Report, *Building Civilian Capacity for U.S. Stability Operations: The Rule of Law Component,* by Michael Dziedzic, Robert Perito, and Beth DeGrasse (2004).

[12] These include the International Criminal Investigative Training Assistance Program (ICITAP) and Office of Overseas Prosecutorial Development, Assistance, and Training (OPDAT) programs.

jointly to the new undersecretary of state and USAID administrator. He or she would supervise the agency's stabilization and reconstruction activities, some of which are currently undertaken through several USAID functional and regional bureaus (each of which now reports to an assistant administrator). The Task Force also recommends expanding USAID's Office of Transition Initiatives (OTI) to enhance existing programs for economic assistance, reform of indigenous institutions, quick impact projects, disarmament, demobilization, and reintegration. The expanded office also would be responsible for constructing an information management system to share critical information with appropriate U.S. government agencies, including the military, during the post-conflict operations.

Fully fund the planned "Active Response Corps" to provide needed civilian manpower and the opportunity for Americans to serve their country abroad. To support the aforementioned stabilization activities, the president has asked the State Department to develop a new corps comprised of volunteers with relevant expertise, to serve as "first responders" in crises. The Task Force supports this step, which is drawn from the legislative proposal of Senators Lugar and Biden, and would ultimately provide the personnel the State Department and USAID would need to fulfill the recommendations outlined in this report. However, the corps must be fully funded and work in tandem with USAID to avoid duplication of effort.

Beyond the State Department and USAID

Establish coordinators for reconstruction-related programs in other agencies, including the Departments of Treasury, Commerce, Agriculture, Labor, and Health and Human Services. A number of civilian agencies have technical expertise that is especially relevant in a post-conflict environment. At the Treasury Department, ad hoc task forces were eliminated, and, in early 2005, a new standing Task Force for Financial Reconstruction and Stabilization was created to feed into the interagency planning process. This is crucial, as the speedy deployment of economic reconstruction assistance is a critical first step in stabilization efforts in conjunction with political and military planning. At the other agencies, creating a single point of contact will help the State Department's coordination efforts.[13]

Strengthen the capacity of the Intelligence Community to provide timely and effective information relating to the requirements of stabilization and reconstruction operations. The intelligence community (IC) could play a larger role in supporting stabilization efforts. Predicting post-conflict conditions and their impact on U.S. policy should be part of the intelligence assessment process. This will require the full range of collection capabilities, including human reporting, signals intelligence, and imagery. The intentions and capabilities of parties in conflict, and the level of skills and motivation of civil servants, religious, and community leaders who will bear the brunt of the burden of rebuilding society and its infrastructure, are vital to understanding how the United States can operate in a post-conflict environment. In recent years, the IC has responded to requirements in this area on an ad hoc basis, too often resulting in the deployment of insufficiently trained personnel. In addition, issues relating to stabilization and reconstruction operations are scattered across several offices within each intelligence agency, increasing the challenge of preparing timely and effective intelligence.

Therefore, the Task Force recommends ***the establishment of a cell under the newly created Deputy Director of National Intelligence for Collection to improve the IC's collection and analysis on weak and failed states.*** This unit would be the focal point for planning, developing training and doctrine, and assisting with reconstruction intelligence operations. The unit would also review collection requirements and implement community-wide collection strategies to accelerate the flow of useful information to decision-makers. On the analytical side, pol-icymakers need stronger analytical products to give them a clearer

---

[13]Of course, each of these agencies has been involved in post-conflict reconstruction missions in the past, playing a critical role in helping to stabilize the economy. For example, in Iraq U.S. Department of Agriculture (USDA) expert Dan Amstutz (appointed U.S. senior ministry adviser for agriculture by the agriculture secretary) worked on reconstruction of the agricultural sector with a number of partners, including USAID, the Coalition Provisional Authority, and the Australian government. Our recommendations are designed to enhance the capacity of agencies to play this kind of role.

picture of various post-conflict dynamics. We also recommend the creation of ad hoc National Intelligence Officers (NIOs), who would focus on stabilization intelligence requirements related to specific crises and press for authoritative analysis from the IC on a rapid basis.

It should be noted that there will be inevitable disagreements between the intelligence and the political and military personnel with expertise in the region. Some of this disagreement arises from a lack of trained personnel familiar with the language, culture, and customs of the area, as is evident in Iraq and Afghanistan. The intelligence community recognizes that it, too, must increase its ability to gain human intelligence on the ground with highly trained officers.

International Financing of Stabilization and Reconstruction

In every post-conflict mission, ensuring that the "trains are running and the lights are on"—that is, providing essential services—is a top reconstruction priority. Such services are a prerequisite for the rehabilitation of the economy, and the failure to repair basic infrastructure always has serious negative political consequences. Though many governments and international organizations have developed quick-impact programs to jump-start small-scale projects, the larger capital construction projects are subject to slow and cumbersome processes.

A core problem is raising money through donor conferences. While the impact of failing infrastructure is felt from day one, these conferences take too much time to pull together. Further, it often takes donor countries an unacceptably long time to fulfill their pledges, since, as in the case of the United States, many rely on budget supplementals to appropriate these funds. The result is lost opportunities.

Another problem is coordinating the reconstruction assistance offered by national governments, regional organizations, and international financial institutions. Too often, there is an overlap of effort in some areas and insufficient aid in others. In recognition of this challenge, an important aspect of the UN secretary-general's proposed Peace Building Commission would be to better integrate coordination between the UN and the international financial institutions.[14]

[14] A Peace Building Commission was proposed in the Report of the Secretary-General's High-Level Panel (HLP) on Threats, Challenges and Change.

28

Push to create a standing multilateral reconstruction Trust Fund, managed under the auspices of the Group of Eight (G8) industrialized nations.
This fund would supplement bilateral aid such as the State Department reserve fund recommended in this report. The new fund would be capitalized at approximately $1 billion and managed by a donor board consisting of representatives from the G8 member states, the UN, the World Bank, and other contributing countries. Placing the trust fund under the auspices of the G8 would allow for more flexible and timely disbursement of funds, compared to the relatively cumbersome International Financial Institutions (IFIs) legal restrictions and administrative requirements. Its sole focus would be high-priority projects during the first year and certain critical recurring expenditures (such as supporting salaries and maintaining local government institutions). It would not replace the existing donors' conferences but would act as a bridge to solve the time-lags associated with coordinating and securing donor assistance. As donor country pledges materialize, the fund would be replenished.

Further, when a particular stabilization and reconstruction mission is underway, a country-specific national fund could be created using a percentage of trust fund monies along with funds from other nations and institutions with available capital. These national funds would be modeled loosely after the Afghanistan Reconstruction Trust Fund (ARTF), though with more flexibility than typically associated with the disbursement of World Bank monies.[15]

---

[15] The ARTF is one of the key structures available to the Afghan government to finance key reconstruction activities. Formally established in 2002, it is jointly managed by the World Bank, UN Development Programme (UNDP), Asian Development Bank (ADB), and the Islamic Development Bank but requires the active participation and leadership of the Afghan government. As of mid-2004, the ARTF had received over $550 million in contributions, with disbursements of approximately $350 million. A management committee meets regularly to review disbursements and, once approved, the Afghan government contracts with an implementing partner (an NGO, a UN agency, or a private organization) to fulfill the project. Priorities are set jointly by the fund's managers and the Afghan Government and can be financed independently or co-financed with other World Bank entities or donor-supported projects. The trust fund does not allow for earmarking of expenditures in order to maximize efficiency and to address the highest priority projects, though donors can indicate a preference about how they would like contributions to be spent.

The United Nations

Peacekeeping was not envisioned in the original UN Charter. It evolved shortly after the founding of the UN under Chapter VI of the Charter, which authorizes UN action to promote the peaceful settlement of disputes with the consent of the parties. From the UN's inception until the late 1980s, most peacekeeping operations involved deployment of very lightly armed UN troops to monitor ceasefires or disengagement agreements between states. In those forty years, there were just thirteen such operations, beginning with the UN Truce Supervision Organization in the Middle East in 1948 and continuing through the UN Interim Force in Lebanon that was first deployed in 1978.

With the end of the Cold War, the United States and the other UN Security Council (UNSC) members sought to transform the role of the United Nations in peacekeeping and post-conflict reconstruction. After 1988, member states pushed the UN to undertake more complex operations aimed at resolving internal conflicts, the related political transition process, and post-conflict reconstruction.[16] In general, these operations operated with the consent of the parties, though peacekeepers sometimes faced the threat of oppositionists. A second evolution began in 1993, with the deployment of U.S.-led peace "enforcement" forces in Somalia. Operating as UNOSOM II, the force was a UN mission, acting under Chapter VII of the UN Charter, which authorizes UN intervention irrespective of whether the parties to the conflict consent to the deployments.

[16] UN operations in Namibia, Central America, and Cambodia exemplified this new focus.

30

On many occasions in the 1990s, UNSC-mandated peacekeeping operations were inadequate to prevent outbreaks of violence and political upheaval. One of the lessons of the ultimate failure of the Somalia deployment was that UN-led blue-helmeted forces, even when supported by highly sophisticated militaries, are insufficient when considerable violent opposition is expected. As a result, subsequent UN missions in Bosnia, Kosovo, East Timor, and Afghanistan included forcible entry into the countries to enforce the peace. Those very demanding actions were fulfilled by green-helmeted military forces deployed under national and regional commands. Despite UNSC awareness of the limitations of UN military operations, the Security Council continues to deploy forces into very challenging environments marked by violence and even combat.[17]

Unprecedented Needs and Challenges

As the United Nations approaches its sixtieth anniversary, demand for UN involvement in stabilization and reconstruction missions is straining the organization. The UNSC continues to authorize peacekeeping missions, outpacing the capacity of the institution to keep up with mission requirements. Troop and personnel requirements often exceed the numbers that member states are willing to contribute, while failed states spiral into chaos and mass killings remain unanswered. Longstanding proposals to "reform" the UN capacity remain partially implemented and deserve more serious attention from UN member states. Without effective reform, critical gaps will remain, hobbling the UN's ability to fulfill its mandates. Finally, criminal acts by troops serving under the UN flag have victimized the people UN forces are meant to protect and tarnished the larger reputation of the institution.

The secretary-general has appointed panels in recent years to consider these issues in detail. The first was the Panel on United Nations Peace Operations (also known as the Brahimi report) in 2000. The High-Level Panel on Threats, Challenges and Change issued a report in

---

[17] This has been the case, for example, in Sierra Leone, the Democratic Republic of the Congo, Burundi, and Haiti, and the UNSC has authorized the use of force so peacekeepers can defend both themselves and their mandate.

December 2004. The secretary-general made his own recommendations in March 2005 for states to consider in preparations for the
Millennium Summit in September 2005. Each has made serious and
wide-ranging recommendations on the conduct of operations, including
how the UN headquarters and field missions work, the allocation
of resources, and the role of member countries in supporting these
operations.

Though some important progress has been made,[18] it is unclear
whether the UN can shoulder these formidable responsibilities without
a fundamental change in approach and significantly increased resources.
In considering the challenges facing the UN, the Task Force has agreed
on several recommendations that should guide the UN reform effort,
recognizing that U.S. leadership is crucial.

Play to the UN's Strengths

*The Task Force believes the UN Secretariat and Department of
Peacekeeping Operations is best suited to focus on mission planning,
training, and developing operational standards, which will improve the*

---

[18] Some progress on the reform agenda has been made. The secretariat has increased the use
of fact-finding missions and has been far more frank in describing requirements and limitations
relating to peace operations to the council. The UN Stand-by Arrangements System has been
reorganized and the UNSC approved the use of "planning mandates," after which the secretary-
general could canvass governments for troop contributions—with implementation theoretically
delayed until adequate troops are identified. Further, the Department of Peacekeeping Operations (DPKO) staff was increased, giving the organization greater capacity to anticipate, organize,
support, and manage the range of peace operations required by the Security Council. DPKO
also has developed an on-call list for deployment of military personnel to headquarters staff.
Finally, DPKO has introduced sixteen "Standard Generic Training Modules" for troop-
contributing nations. Organizationally, there also have been a number of reform efforts to try
to improve UN effectiveness, such as the separation of planning and support for military and
civilian police operations. Also, in some instances, the UN has "dual-hatted" the senior
development official as a deputy Special Representative of the Secretary-General (SRSG) and
co-located other parts of the UN country team in the office of the SRSG to enhance ground-
level coordination. In New York, establishment of Integrated Mission Task Forces (IMTFs)
has increased coordination within the United Nations through working groups for specific
peacekeeping missions, and these task forces serve as a forum for the discussion of issues. See
The Brahimi Report and the Future of Peace Operations, by William J. Durch, Victoria K. Holt,
Caroline R. Earle, and Moira K. Shanahan, the Henry L. Stimson Center, Washington, DC,
December 2003 (www.stimson.org/fopo), for further details.

interoperability and effectiveness of national forces operating in a multilateral environment.

Today, participants in UN missions—be they the mission's leadership, participating national contingents, or volunteers—are deployed with widely varying skills, often forcing the UN to struggle to shore up significant operational weaknesses in a crisis environment. A primary focus of the UN should be promoting "best practices" and leading training programs that can achieve minimum levels of capacity. Also, given heightened security risks, systems for integrating real-time information and intelligence are needed. The UN is particularly well-placed to help develop these core competencies, which would redound to the benefit of all nations participating in UN-authorized operations.

As missions are defined, the UN must send well-equipped, motivated, and highly trained military forces in order to fulfill its peacekeeping mandates. This is no easy task, but it begins with a clearer and more honest division of labor between the UN and national governments. Member states must recognize that many UNSC-authorized missions may be more appropriately led by green-helmeted national forces than blue-helmeted ones.

Align and Increase Resources

The UN is experiencing an unprecedented growth in peacekeeping operations due to new and continuing missions in Haiti, Côte d'Ivoire, East Timor, Liberia, and Sierra Leone, as well as other new missions.[19] Given this surge in demand, the international community runs the risk of failure if minimum resource and personnel levels are not provided to support these missions. The practice of the Security Council directing the UN Secretariat to organize complex, multidimensional peace operations without sufficiently funding or supporting their mandates must end. To address this continuing problem, the Task Force makes the following set of recommendations.

---

[19] In addition, there are new missions in Burundi and southern Sudan and a likely mission in the Darfur region of Sudan, as well as a considerable expansion of the already-sizeable mission in the Democratic Republic of the Congo.

Link Security Council mission approval to resource allocations. It is clear the overall requirement of about $4 billion in assessed peacekeeping contributions will continue to rise. The UNSC should acknowledge the financial strain by limiting the number of new and expanded peacekeeping missions until contributing nations increase their financial commitments. Further, to increase the number of trained troops and material for such operations, the UNSC should refrain from finalizing any new missions until the proper numbers of peacekeepers and related equipment are identified. The United States and its allies must contribute their fair share of contingents for peacekeeping operations while supporting UN training efforts aimed at developing country troops.[20] Some argue that political support for missions might wane if member nations are slow to assemble peacekeepers and other material support, but in the Task Force's view, it is better to get it right than do it fast.

Establish an assessment schedule for member state contributions to nonsecurity, post-conflict reconstruction activities. Today, there is no consistent way to fund the programs most critical to achieving mission success (including disarmament, demobilization and reintegration, justice and reconciliation, and institution-building), despite the recognition that they are crucial to winning the peace. An assessment schedule, similar to ones used for peacekeeping operations, would help solve this problem.

Create a small corps at UN headquarters to organize deployment of civilian police and develop national pools of candidates to speed these deployments. This step would help address the unacceptably slow deployment of civilian police to peacekeeping missions, which has repeatedly hampered UN operations. With a small team of fifty to one hundred police experts, the UN could fill a crucial gap in capability.

Convene a special session on peacekeeping and reconstruction requirements for the coming two years. This annual meeting would review

---

[20] It is noteworthy that the top contributing countries to UN peace operations are from Asia and Africa and that no developed country is among the top twenty contributors. The United States provides roughly less than 1 percent of UN peacekeepers, and the majority of that contribution is civilian police.

ongoing peacekeeping missions and develop a projection of requirements for the upcoming two years. Such a meeting would also include
a statement of determination by member states to meet their obligations.

Peace-Building Commission

***Support the creation of a Peace-Building Commission, advocated by the
recent UN High-Level Panel.*** This commission will maintain a focus
on the mission, the efficiency of operations, and endurance of the
commitment of member nations. Secretary-General Kofi Annan
endorsed this commission as a solution to mission fatigue, since it will
support specific post-conflict missions past the initial flurry of activity
and interest.

Support the reintroduction of the gratis personnel system (whereby member states loan their own national experts to work in UN positions).
This will help improve DPKO effectiveness, particularly in contingency
and operational planning and logistics support. The UN eliminated its
gratis system in 1997 because of concerns it distorted staffing arrangements in favor of wealthy countries. While there are legitimate issues
associated with ensuring equal and fair representation, the system was
very valuable in providing expertise and instilling a sense of ownership
by troop-contributing states in the planning and operational aspects of
UN peace-building operations.

Insist on Accountability

***Support the development of specific guidelines for contributing countries
to UN peacekeeping mission, including a code of conduct and pledges
to screen, train, and, where necessary, discipline such troops, police, or
civilian employees who violate those guidelines.*** UN peacekeeping is
coming under greater scrutiny because of the criminal behavior of some
troops operating under the UN flag. Contributing countries should
agree to cooperate fully with UN investigations of conduct and to take
rapid action to remove abusive members.

Regional Organizations

Developing stabilization and reconstruction capabilities within regional organizations such as NATO or the African Union is also important. There is a pressing need to increase the overall number of well-trained and well-equipped peacekeepers. The large majority of UN peacekeepers are now in Africa, and African governments have the greatest interest and incentive to contribute to such operations. However, they also have the greatest need for train-and-equip programs to enable them to undertake additional responsibilities. It is in the interest of the United States to develop military peacekeeping capacity in other nations.

Africa, in particular, would benefit from such a regional force. The African Union plans to build five subregional brigades for this purpose. The G8 nations are training as many as 75,000 peacekeepers worldwide over the next five to six years. The Bush administration said it would seek an additional $660 million to train and equip peacekeepers through the Global Peace Operations Initiative, starting in Africa. Several European governments are expanding ongoing training and support for deployments in sub-Saharan Africa.[21] The U.S. Congress funded the first year of the Bush administration's proposal at $80 million. The United States should increase funding for this initiative and support

[21]At the African Union's Maputo Summit in July 2003, African heads of state put forward a proposal for an African Peace Facility intended to support African peacekeeping operations on the African continent. In March 2004, the European Commission announced support of 250 million euros (US$300 million) from the European Development Fund to support the initiative.

efforts by African multinational organizations to develop their own capacities to organize and deploy effective peace operations.

Beyond Africa, both NATO and the European Union have launched new initiatives to develop stabilization capabilities. At the June 2004 NATO Summit, the alliance vowed to improve and adapt its operational capabilities to better deal with challenges such as stabilization activities outside its traditional theatre of operations.[22] NATO said it would increase its commitment to the International Security Assistance Force (ISAF) in Afghanistan, in part through the introduction of provincial reconstruction teams (PRTs).[23] For its part, the European Union is developing its capacity to deploy military forces and civilians for stabilization and reconstruction operations. The European Union assumed control from NATO of the peacekeeping mission in Bosnia in December 2004. There are also EU police support missions in Bosnia and Macedonia and an EU rule of law mission in Georgia.

Provide full support for initiatives to train regional peacekeeping contingents and civilian police. This includes increased contributions to the voluntary peacekeeping account. The administration should include full funding for the G8 initiative in future budgets, as well as increased funding for the voluntary peacekeeping account of the United Nations. The administration requested and received funding of about $104 million for this account in 2005. Given ongoing needs in Africa alone, this contribution should be doubled in 2006.

Promote dialogue with governments such as Australia, India, Brazil, and Argentina to encourage broader cooperation on peacekeeping capacity. These and other governments have demonstrated significant capabilities in stabilization and reconstruction activities, and their skills and expertise could play an important role in encouraging more effective involvement by states in their regions.

---

[22] For the full statement of commitments, see the Istanbul Summit communiqué, at http://www.nato.int/docu/pr/2004/p04-096e.htm.
[23] PRTs, composed of civilian and military personnel, are deployed to Afghanistan's provinces to provide security for aid workers and assist in reconstruction work.

Conclusion

This report is being issued in a year when a series of international conferences are being hosted to help some of the world's poorest nations, particularly in Africa. Rich nations have pledged to increase aid and forgive the debt of these countries, as well as to revise international trade laws to help them permanently climb out of poverty by selling their goods and services in the global marketplace.

Against this backdrop, the Task Force report represents the other side of the story. In failed states with ongoing conflict and terrorist footholds, these economic and political improvements will never be realized. Where conflict has been followed by inattention and unmet promises, violence reappears and spreads through the region. Military advantages are lost in chaos and corruption.

The United States, with history's most powerful armed forces, need not squander its victories with poor post-war planning. As the world shrinks and the problems of distant neighbors explode in our own backyards, this has become an urgent issue. Whether fighting against terrorism, in support of democracy or to protect human rights, the United States can no longer afford to mount costly military actions and then treat peacekeeping with anything less than the same seriousness of purpose.

Underlying this report is the realization that peacekeeping and reconstruction should be seen as conflict prevention done late. The more successful the diplomatic and development efforts to prevent and mitigate conflict, the less likely it would be that the United States will be called to embark on these difficult and costly post-conflict missions.

With the national attention focused on how to secure the peace in post-war Iraq, these recommendations are not only timely but, we hope, a lasting answer to how to preserve American principles and power.

Additional or Dissenting Views

I want to register my concern about three matters on which the Task Force did not focus. First, while the United States needs to give increased attention and support to post-conflict stabilization and reconstruction, we must also give higher priority to the diplomacy and development that will prevent conflict in the first place. Second, we must recognize just how difficult and long-term post-conflict nation-building can be. The measures that the Task Force proposes are important and can make a positive difference, but there are no guarantees. We must carefully consider the hazards and costs of post-conflict stabilization and reconstruction before going to war. Finally, the Task Force rightly advocated for increased post-conflict coordination between military and civilian agencies, but did not explore the dangers of blurring the lines between military-political and humanitarian actors, for whom independence and impartiality are critical.

Peter D. Bell

The emphasis on initial pre-intervention planning for post-conflict stabilization and reconstruction is the most important "takeaway" of this report. Governmental structure to support interagency civil-military planning is important, but restructuring alone will not guarantee effective practice without commitment, training, and extensive practice.

Antonia Handler Chayes

41

I fully endorse the thrust of this report, including its main recommendations. The Task Force is especially correct in recommending that "building America's capability to conduct stabilization and reconstruction operations . . . be a top foreign policy priority." Unfortunately, some organizational recommendations do not adequately reflect this priority. This is especially the case with the Task Force's proposals on the reorganization of the National Security Council. Since stabilization and reconstruction is the kind of issue that requires the active involvement and participation of many agencies of the U.S. government, the effectiveness of such operations depends critically on how well the White House and the NSC manage the tasks of policy development, coordination, and oversight. The recommendation to appoint another senior director and create a directorate to undertake these tasks is necessary, but not sufficient. To be accorded the right priority, it is necessary to make this a deputy-level responsibility—with a deputy national security adviser in charge.

Whether we like it or not, there has been a steady proliferation of deputy national security advisers. Under Condoleezza Rice, the NSC ended up having five deputies, a practice that has continued, in different form, under Stephen Hadley. To have an organizational structure that puts deputy national security advisers in charge of democracy-promotion, counterterrorism, international economic policy, Iraq and Afghanistan, and strategic communication, but not stabilization and reconstruction operations, leaves an important organizational mission unfulfilled and rightly raises questions about the degree to which building capacity for such operations is "a top foreign policy priority."

Ivo H. Daalder
joined by
Susan E. Rice

I would have liked to see greater emphasis in this excellent report on the desirability of greater American participation in UN peacekeeping operations. At present, among the 58,843 UN soldiers serving in sixteen trouble spots around the world, ten are American. One might plead the competing demands of Afghanistan and Iraq, but the number of Americans committed to UN operations was no higher before those two operations began. Since the late 1990's, indeed, the United States has taken the position that the world's only superpower does not do peacekeeping. And, unfortunately, America's principal allies have begun to follow Washington's burden-shedding example. Of the 58,843 UN troops on duty today, only eighteen are German, nine Norwegian, eight Dutch, and two Belgian.

Despite the UN's almost exclusive reliance upon less well-equipped Third World troops for many of its missions, these operations have proved remarkably effective in forestalling renewed conflict and setting war-torn societies on the path to democratic government. Indeed, the UN record for nation-building compares quite favorably with that of the United States. Of course, the two are inextricably linked. American successes in places like Kosovo and Afghanistan have depended heavily on UN support, and UN successes in places like East Timor and Sierra Leone have depended upon American. But coalitions of the willing are generally much more costly and difficult to organize than UN peacekeeping missions, and should be the option of last resort, not the first. In marginal situations, where only a slightly more potent force would allow the UN to cope with a difficult situation, the United States and its principal allies would be better off contributing forces to a UN-led operation than trying to organize one of their own. The current situation in Haiti is a good example of where only a small admixture of American troops would greatly increase the credibility and effectiveness of an otherwise faltering UN peacekeeping operation.

James F. Dobbins
joined by
Jock Covey,
Susan E. Rice, and
Kenneth Roth

I strongly endorse the report's primary recommendations but believe further consideration is needed regarding placement of the proposed multilateral reconstruction trust fund under the auspice of the Group of Eight (G8) rather than within the proposed Peacebuilding Fund at the UN, which would be consistent with the report's recommendations for a strengthened UN coordinating and operational role. My reasoning is two-fold. First, there is no guarantee that a G8-operated fund would be any more flexible and timely than one at the UN (e.g., UNDP-World Bank experience in Afghanistan) or at the World Bank (e.g., the Holst Fund for the Palestine Authority's recurrent payments was managed in a timely and flexible way—the initial start up time was the problem). Second, a UN-based Peacebuilding Fund would presumably attract a broader range of contributors, including, importantly, the Nordic countries, who are less likely to contribute to a trust fund at the G8 over which they would have little if any decisional authority.

Shepard L. Forman
joined by
James F. Dobbins

The report constitutes both a generally informed and useful analysis of the problem and a constructive and practical set of recommendations. I have, however, reservations on two points—one related to the analysis, the other to the recommendations.

A great gulf lies between situations—like Iraq and Somalia—where there is continuing active combat aimed at least in part at the international effort and those—like post-Dayton Bosnia and East Timor after the Indonesian withdrawal—where there is not. The report acknowledges that post-conflict recovery is more difficult in the former context than the latter, but it does not give sufficient attention to the scale of that increased difficulty, which amounts to a difference in kind and not merely in degree. Not only is progress much more difficult when there is active armed interference, but the appropriate chain of command, priorities for action, and methods of applying resources differ drastically. Broadly speaking, the report's recommendations seem better attuned to the case of a relatively benign environment than to one where there is active armed resistance.

The report recommends establishing separate, high-level offices in the National Security Council, the State Department, and the Office of the Secretary of Defense for post-conflict reconstruction. There is certainly a need for greater operational capacity to plan and mobilize resources for the post-conflict phase, but I doubt that creating specialized senior offices will help much in that effort. Indeed, creating separate advocate offices seems to me not only to put excessive confidence in the efficacy of wiring diagram solutions, but to risk perpetuating the attitude that the post-conflict effort is a distinct problem, isolated from both the prevention and combat aspects of dealing with major security problems. The key to success is getting the "core" policymakers who deal with a crisis to work the post-conflict problem—and secure the resources for doing so—and it is far from clear that creating specialized "advocacy" offices will advance that cause. On the contrary, if the necessary specialized and technical planning and implementation staffs are seen as an integral part of the team responsible for general policy and action planning—whether in the White House, State, or Defense Department—they are likely to be more effective than if they are seen as some sort of special interest outside the institutional mainstream. (The model of giving a new state undersecretary overall responsibility for post-conflict matters, but having USAID in charge of implementation, seems particularly problematic.)

Walter B. Slocombe

Task Force Members

Frederick D. Barton is Co-Director of the Post-Conflict Reconstruction Project at the Center for Strategic and International Studies (CSIS) and also serves as Senior Adviser in the International Security Program. Prior to that, he was the UN Deputy High Commissioner for Refugees in Geneva and was the first director of the Office of Transition Initiatives at the U.S. Agency for International Development in Washington, DC.

Peter D. Bell* is President of CARE USA. He was also President of the Edna McConnell Clark Foundation in New York, a Senior Associate at the Carnegie Endowment for International Peace, and President of the Inter-American Foundation, a public agency that supports grassroots development in Latin America and the Caribbean. From 1977 through 1979, he was initially Special Assistant to the Secretary and then Deputy Undersecretary of the U.S. Department of Health, Education, and Welfare.

Samuel R. Berger is Chairman of Stonebridge International, LLC, an international strategic advisory firm based in Washington, DC. Mr. Berger served as National Security Adviser to President William J. Clinton from 1997 to 2000, as Deputy National Security Adviser from 1993 to 1996, and as Deputy Director of the State Department's Policy Planning Staff from 1977 to 1980. Prior to his service as National

Note: Task Force members participate in their individual and not institutional capacities.
* The individual has endorsed the report and submitted an additional or a dissenting view.

47

Security Adviser, Mr. Berger spent sixteen years with the Washington law firm of Hogan and Hartson, where he headed the firm's international group.

Henry S. Bienen has been President of Northwestern University since 1995. Prior to his current appointment, he was James S. McDonnell Distinguished University Professor and Dean of the Woodrow Wilson School of Public and International Affairs at Princeton University. President Bienen has been a member of the Institute for Advanced Studies at Princeton University and a Fellow at the Center for Advanced Studies in the Behavioral Sciences at Stanford University. He was a member of the Senior Review Panel at the Central Intelligence Agency and has been a consultant to the U.S. Department of State, the National Security Council, USAID, the World Bank, and many other corporations and foundations.

Hans Binnendijk holds the Theodore Roosevelt Chair in National Security Policy and is Director of the Center for Technology and National Security Policy at the National Defense University. He previously served on the National Security Council as Special Assistant to the President and Senior Director for Defense Policy and Arms Control, and as Principal Deputy Director of the State Department's Policy Planning Staff. Mr. Binnendijk also served as Deputy Staff Director of the Senate Foreign Relations Committee.

Antonia Handler Chayes* is Visiting Professor of International Politics and Law at the Fletcher School of Law and Diplomacy, Tufts University. She chairs the Project on International Institutions and Conflict Management of the Program on Negotiation at the Harvard Law School. Professor Chayes was Vice Chair and Senior Consultant of Conflict Management Group (CMG), a nonprofit international dispute resolution organization. During the Carter administration, she was Assistant and later Undersecretary of the U.S. Air Force.

Jock Covey* is a Senior Vice President of Bechtel Corporation. He served in Kosovo as a Principal Deputy at the UN Mission in Kosovo

(UNMIK) and in Bosnia as Deputy High Representative. A career Foreign Service Officer, he also served twice at the National Security Council as Special Assistant to the President for Near Eastern and South Asian affairs in the Reagan administration and for Implementation of the Dayton Peace Accords in the Clinton administration.

Ivo H. Daalder* is a Senior Fellow in Foreign Policy Studies at the Brookings Institution, where he also holds the Sydney Stein Jr. Chair in International Security. He is a frequent commentator on current affairs and has authored ten books. From 1995 to 1996, Dr. Daalder served as Director for European Affairs on President William J. Clinton's National Security Council staff, where he was responsible for coordinating U.S. policy toward Bosnia.

James F. Dobbins* is Director of the International Security and Defense Policy Center at the RAND Corporation. He has held State Department and White House posts, including Assistant Secretary of State for Europe, Special Assistant to the President for the Western Hemisphere, Special Adviser to the President and Secretary of State for the Balkans, and Ambassador to the European Community. Mr. Dobbins has handled a variety of crisis management assignments as the Clinton administration's special envoy for Somalia, Haiti, Bosnia, and Kosovo; and the George W. Bush administration's first special envoy for Afghanistan. He is principal author of the two-volume RAND publication *History of Nation-Building*.

Shepard L. Forman* has been Director of the Center on International Cooperation at New York University since 1996. Prior to founding the Center, he was Director of International Affairs Programs and Director of Human Rights and Governance Programs at the Ford Foundation. He is co-editor, with Stewart Patrick, of *Good Intentions: Pledges of Aid to Countries Emerging from Conflict* and *Multilateralism and U.S. Foreign Policy: Ambivalent Engagement*.

Bob Graham served as U.S. Senator from Florida from 1987 to 2005. He was Chair of the Senate Intelligence Committee from 2001 to

2003 and Chair of the Democratic Senatorial Campaign Committee from 1993 to 1995. Prior to his election to the U.S. Senate, he was Governor of Florida and a State Senator. Senator Graham is author, with Jeff Nussbaum, of *Intelligence Matters: The CIA, the FBI, Saudi Arabia, and the Failure of America's War on Terror.*

Chuck Hagel is Nebraska's senior U.S. Senator and is serving his second term in the Senate. He is Chairman of the Senate Foreign Relations International Economic Policy, Export, and Trade Promotion Subcommittee and of the Senate Banking Securities and Investment Subcommittee. Senator Hagel also serves on the Intelligence Committee, Rules Committee, and the Banking, Housing, and Urban Affairs Committee.

John J. Hamre was elected President and Chief Executive Officer of the Center for Strategic and International Studies (CSIS) in January 2000. He came to CSIS from the Defense Department, where he served as Deputy Secretary of Defense from 1997 to 1999 and as Undersecretary of Defense (Comptroller) from 1993 to 1997. Dr. Hamre also worked for ten years as a Professional Staff Member of the Senate Armed Services Committee. From 1978 to 1984, he served in the Congressional Budget Office, where he became Deputy Assistant Director for National Security and International Affairs.

Jane Harman is in her sixth term representing the Thirty-sixth Congressional District of California. She is the Senior Democrat on the Permanent Select Committee on Intelligence and a senior member of the Homeland Security Committee. She previously served on the Armed Services Committee, the Science Committee, and is currently on leave from the Energy and Commerce Committee. Previously, Harman served in the White House as Deputy Secretary of the Cabinet, as Special Counsel at the Department of Defense, as an attorney in private law practice, and as Regent Professor at the University of California at Los Angeles. In 2000, she was a member of the National Commission on Terrorism (the Bremer Commission). In 1998, Harman was a candidate for Governor of California.

Robert D. Hormats is Vice Chairman of Goldman Sachs (International) and Managing Director of Goldman, Sachs and Co. He served as a senior staff member for international economic affairs on the National Security Council from 1969 to 1977, during which time he was Senior Economic Adviser to Henry A. Kissinger, Brent Scowcroft, and Zbigniew Brzezinski. He also served as Senior Deputy Assistant Secretary of State for Economic and Business Affairs, Ambassador and Deputy U.S. Trade Representative, and Assistant Secretary of State for Economic and Business Affairs.

David A. Lipton is Managing Director and head of Global Country Risk Management at Citigroup. He joined Citigroup following five years at Moore Capital Management. He served in the Treasury Department during the Clinton administration from 1993 to 1998 as Undersecretary for International Affairs and before that as Assistant Secretary, where he designed and implemented U.S. policy to assist East European countries in their transition to market economies.

William L. Nash is the General John W. Vessey Senior Fellow for Conflict Prevention and the Director of Center for Preventive Action at the Council on Foreign Relations.

Susan E. Rice* is a Senior Fellow in Foreign Policy at the Brookings Institution. From 1997 to 2001, she was Assistant Secretary of State for African Affairs. Before joining the State Department, Ms. Rice served at the White House as Special Assistant to the President and Senior Director for African Affairs and was Director for International Organizations and Peacekeeping at the National Security Council.

David Rieff is Senior Fellow at the World Policy Institute at the New School University and at the New York Institute for the Humanities of New York University. He is a widely published author on issues such as humanitarian aid. His books include *Slaughterhouse: Bosnia and the Failure of the West* and *A Bed for the Night: Humanitarianism in Crisis*.

Kenneth Roth* is the Executive Director of Human Rights Watch, a post he has held since 1993. From 1987 to 1993, Mr. Roth served as Deputy Director of the organization. Previously, he was a federal prosecutor for the U.S. Attorney's Office for the Southern District of New York and the Iran-Contra investigation in Washington, DC. He also worked in private practice as a litigator. Mr. Roth has conducted human rights investigations around the globe.

Eric P. Schwartz was on the National Security Council staff from 1993 to 2001, where he finished his tenure as Special Assistant to the President and Senior Director for Multilateral and Humanitarian Affairs. He served as the second-ranking official at the Office of the United Nations High Commissioner for Human Rights in 2003-2004, and has also worked as a staff consultant at the House Foreign Affairs Committee, as a Senior Fellow at the Council on Foreign Relations and the United States Institute of Peace, and as Washington Director of Asia Watch (now Human Rights Watch/Asia).

Brent Scowcroft is President and founder of the Scowcroft Group. General Scowcroft served as National Security Adviser to both Presidents Gerald Ford and George H. W. Bush. His twenty-nine-year military career began with graduation from West Point and concluded with the rank of Lieutenant General following service as the Deputy National Security Adviser. General Scowcroft's Air Force service included Office of the Secretary of Defense International Security Assistance, Special Assistant to the Director of the Joint Chiefs of Staff, and Military Assistant to President Richard Nixon.

Michael A. Sheehan is Deputy Commissioner in the Counterterrorism Bureau at the New York Police Department. He was formerly Assistant Secretary-General for Logistics, Management, and Mine Action Service in the UN Department of Peacekeeping Operations. Before that, Mr. Sheehan served at the State Department as Ambassador-at-Large and Coordinator for Counterterrorism, and as Deputy Assistant Secretary in the Bureau of International Organizations. From 1995 to 1997, he was Director of Global Issues and Multilateral Affairs at the National Security Council.

Walter B. Slocombe* is a member of the Washington, DC, law firm Caplin and Drysdale. He was Undersecretary of Defense for Policy in the Clinton administration and served as Senior Adviser for National Security and Defense in the Coalition Provisional Authority for Iraq.

Gordon R. Sullivan is President of the Association of the U.S. Army. From 1991 to 1995, he was the thirty-second Chief of Staff of the U.S. Army. General Sullivan has served in a variety of command and staff positions, including four years in joint and allied assignments. His overseas assignments include four tours in Europe, two in Vietnam, and one in Korea. General Sullivan also served in assignments on the Army Staff in Washington, DC, including a tour as the Deputy Chief of Staff for Operations and Plans and as the Vice Chief of Staff of the Army. He also serves as a member of the Joint Chiefs of Staff.

Mona K. Sutphen is Managing Director of Stonebridge International, LLC. Previously, she was vice president at Currenex, an institutional foreign-exchange trading platform. A Foreign Service Officer from 1991 to 2000, she served at the National Security Council, the U.S. Mission to the United Nations, and in the Office of the High Representative on civilian implementation of the Bosnia Peace Agreement.

Fareed Zakaria is Editor of *Newsweek International* and writes a regular column for *Newsweek*. His 2003 book, *The Future of Freedom*, was a *New York Times* best-seller and is being translated into eighteen languages. He is a political commentator for ABC News and is the host of PBS's "Foreign Exchange." Dr. Zakaria previously was managing editor of *Foreign Affairs*.

Task Force Observers

Max Boot
Council on Foreign Relations

Dallas C. Brown III
U.S. Department of Defense

Bathsheba N. Crocker
United Nations

James H. Fall III
U.S. Department of Treasury

Judith Kipper
Council on Foreign Relations

James Kunder
U.S. Agency for International Development

Marcel Lettre
Office of Senator Harry Reid (D-NV)

Mary Locke
Senate Committee on Foreign Relations

Barry F. Lowenkron
U.S. Department of State

Jane Holl Lute
United Nations

Johanna Mendelson-Forman
United Nations Foundation

Thant Myint-U
United Nations

Stewart M. Patrick
Center for Global Development

Robin L. Raphel
U.S. Department of State

Joseph Siegle
University of Maryland

Volney James Warner
U.S. Army

Clint Williamson
National Security Council

Selected Reports of Independent Task Forces Sponsored by the Council on Foreign Relations

*†*In Support of Arab Democracy: Why and How* (2005), Madeleine K. Albright and Vin Weber, Co-Chairs; Steven A. Cook, Project Director

*†*Building a North American Community* (2005), John P. Manley, Pedro Aspe, and William F. Weld, Co-Chairs; Thomas P. d'Aquino, Andrés Rozental, and Robert A. Pastor, Vice Chairs; Chappell H. Lawson, Project Director

*†*Iran: Time for a New Approach* (2004), Zbigniew Brzezinski and Robert M. Gates, Co-Chairs; Suzanne Maloney, Project Director

*†*Renewing the Atlantic Partnership* (2004), Henry A. Kissinger and Lawrence H. Summers, Co-Chairs; Charles A. Kupchan, Project Director

*†*Nonlethal Weapons and Capabilities* (2004), Graham T. Allison and Paul X. Kelley, Co-Chairs; Richard L. Garwin, Project Director

*†*New Priorities in South Asia: U.S. Policy Toward India, Pakistan, and Afghanistan* (2003), Frank G.Wisner II, Nicholas Platt, and Marshall M. Bouton, Co-Chairs; Dennis Kux and Mahnaz Ispahani, Project Co-Directors; Cosponsored with the Asia Society

*†*Finding America's Voice: A Strategy for Reinvigorating U.S. Public Diplomacy* (2003), Peter G. Peterson, Chair; Jennifer Sieg, Project Director

*†*Emergency Responders:Drastically Underfunded, Dangerously Unprepared* (2003), Warren B. Rudman, Chair; Richard A. Clarke, Senior Adviser; Jamie F. Metzl, Project Director

*†*Burma:Time for Change* (2003), Mathea Falco, Chair

*†*Meeting the North Korean Nuclear Challenge* (2003), Morton I. Abramowitz and James T. Laney, Co-Chairs; Eric Heginbotham, Project Director

*†*Chinese Military Power* (2003), Harold Brown, Chair; Joseph W. Prueher, Vice Chair; Adam Segal, Project Director

*†*Iraq: The Day After* (2003), Thomas R. Pickering and James R. Schlesinger, Co-Chairs; Eric P. Schwartz, Project Director

*†*Threats to Democracy* (2002), Madeleine K. Albright and Bronislaw Geremek, Co-Chairs; Morton H. Halperin, Project Director; Elizabeth Frawley Bagley, Associate Director

*†*America-Still Unprepared, Still in Danger* (2002), Gary Hart and Warren B. Rudman, Co-Chairs; Stephen Flynn, Project Director

*†*Terrorist Financing* (2002), Maurice R. Greenberg, Chair; William F.Wechsler and Lee S.Wolosky, Project Co-Directors

*†*Enhancing U.S. Leadership at the United Nations* (2002), David Dreier and Lee H. Hamilton, Co-Chairs; Lee Feinstein and Adrian Karatnycky, Project Co-Directors

*†*Testing North Korea: The Next Stage in U.S. and ROK Policy* (2001), Morton I. Abramowitz and James T. Laney, Co-Chairs; Robert A. Manning, Project Director

*†*The United States and Southeast Asia: A Policy Agenda for the New Administration* (2001), J. Robert Kerrey, Chair; Robert A. Manning, Project Director

*†*Strategic Energy Policy: Challenges for the 21st Century* (2001), Edward L. Morse, Chair; Amy Myers Jaffe, Project Director

*†*State Department Reform* (2001), Frank C. Carlucci, Chair; Ian J. Brzezinski, Project Coordinator; Cosponsored with the Center for Strategic and International Studies

*†*U.S.-Cuban Relations in the 21st Century: A Follow-on-Report* (2001), Bernard W. Aronson and William D. Rogers, Co-Chairs; Julia Sweig and Walter Mead, Project Directors

*†*A Letter to the President and a Memorandum on U.S. Policy Toward Brazil* (2001), Stephen Robert, Chair; Kenneth Maxwell, Project Director

*†*Toward Greater Peace and Security in Colombia* (2000), Bob Graham and Brent Scowcroft, Co-Chairs; Michael Shifter, Project Director; Cosponsored with the Inter-American Dialogue

---

†Available on the Council on Foreign Relations website at www.cfr.org.
*Available from Brookings Institution Press. To order, call 800-275-1447.